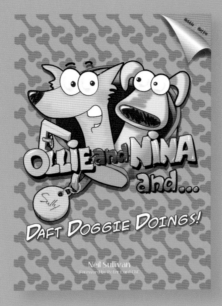

THIS BOOK IS DEDICATED TO
EVERYONE WHO LOVES, CARES FOR, AND
HELPS OUR BELOVED ANIMALS

Hubble & Hattie

Hubble & Hattie

Other great books from Hubble and Hattie and Belvedere –

An often funny, sometimes melancholy, and occasionally accurate guide to understanding the relationship between a dog and a human. A picture book for adults that grew out of one human trying to remember why he ended up with a dog, and sharing his thoughts as pictures on social media.

ISBN: 978-1-787110-00-7

The second volume from Mike&Scrabble explores the growing relationship between a dog and her human through the medium of interpretive dance, illustrated giggles, and pithy one-liners. It's better than *Mike&Scrabble*, because dogs make humans better people.

ISBN: 978-1-787110-60-1

In 2016, much to his surprise, Mr Trump was elected President of the United States of America. This is the story of what happened when Mr Trump went to Washington. The author does not envisage it will end well ...

ISBN: 978-1-787111-63-9

The unique and elegant photographic story of the special bond that exists between dogs and their people: a book about relationships, observed and presented from a dog's point of view. Forty-two incomparable images of four- and two-legged individuals showcase the different dynamics of each relationship.

ISBN: 978-1-845849-85-6

www.hubbleandhattie.com

First published in July 2017 by Veloce Publishing Limited, Veloce House, Parkway Farm Business Park, Middle Farm Way, Poundbury, Dorchester DT1 3AR, England. Fax 01305 250479 / e-mail info@hubbleandhattie.com / web www.hubbleandhattie.com. ISBN: 978-1-787110-65-6 UPC: 6-36847-01065-2.
© 2017 Neil Sullivan and Veloce Publishing. All rights reserved. With the exception of quoting brief passages for the purpose of review, no part of this publication may be recorded, reproduced or transmitted by any means, including photocopying, without the written permission of Veloce Publishing Ltd. Throughout this book logos, model names and designations, etc, have been used for the purposes of identification, illustration and decoration. Such names are the property of the trademark holder as this is not an official publication. Readers with ideas for automotive books, or books on other transport or related hobby subjects, are invited to write to the editorial director of Veloce Publishing at the above address. British Library Cataloguing in Publication Data – A catalogue record for this book is available from the British Library. Typesetting, design and page make-up all by Veloce Publishing Ltd on Apple Mac. Back cover Author caricature by Steven Burke. Printed in India by Parksons Graphics.

Hubble & Hattie

Ollie and NINA and...

DAFT DOGGIE DOINGS!

Neil Sullivan

Foreword by Peter Lord CBE

FOREWORD

Everyone loves a double act.

From Laurel and Hardy to Ant and Dec via Morph and Chas, there's a chemistry that's been proven time and time again. There's something about the misadventures, the misunderstandings, the rivalry – and, ultimately, the love between two mismatched characters – that is always irresistibly fascinating.

So welcome Ollie and Nina, a doggy double act that has it all, and brings laughter to readers while driving the long-suffering Sullivans to despair!

These little cartoons take us into the dogs' world, where every dog owner and dog-lover will finally understand what's going on in those canine brains!

Peter Lord CBE
Co-founder and Creative Director
at Aardman Animation

OLLIE AND NINA AND ...

Together, Ollie and Nina are a classic comedy duo. They have given me endless amounts of material to write and draw about. Now, they star in their very own cartoon strip alongside some of their doggie friends and kitty cat pals. To be honest, these individuals are almost as daft as Ollie and Nina.

Ollie and Nina are both rescue dogs (they rescued us from the sofa). Ollie is a Collie/Saluki cross; Nina is a Whippet/Saluki cross.

We found Ollie online, he was looking for a 'forever home.' He found it with us.

Nina was rescued from kennels in Kuala Lumpur (we lived in Asia for six years). She was frightened, stressed, unhealthy and unhappy. We took her in and made her well, and taught her how to be happy. Now she is very good at being happy, and she spreads joy wherever she goes.

Ollie is all-heart, spontaneous, silly, soppy and loving. He's always busy nosing around and looking for adventures. He loves other dogs and will play with them until they are all played-out!

Nina is thoughtful, wise and gentle. She likes other dogs, especially small ones, but she is very wary of small children. You never really know what's happened to rescue dogs in their past, do you? But we do have a very good idea about her future. It's looking rosy, Nina!

You'll see for yourself just how gifted Ollie and Nina are at being silly in these funny little stories: Ollie and Nina and ...

... enjoy!

...and how I see them.

Ollie and Nina ...

OLLIE and NINA

and... *Ollie and Nina*

CATS!

What is it with cats and dogs?! How come they are such good buddies; why do they love to frolic and play together?

Okay, what crazy, topsy-turvy world do I live in, I hear you ask ... but that's exactly how it is with our little menagerie: honestly, our animals are shameless. We have four cats and two dogs, and I think someone really needs to sit them down and explain the facts of life to them. Don't they know that cats and dogs snuggling up together for an afternoon nap is just plain wrong, even if it is kind of cute.

Every time I witness this freak of nature, I always tease Ollie and Nina that I will rat them out to their best friends. Ollie would be mortified if Flynn, his big, butch Red Setter pal, knew about his feline friends and his sissy goings-on. And Nina would blush to her roots with embarrassment if Bentley, her Working Cocker Spaniel pal, was to sniff out her cosy cat encounters.

Well, they can all rest easy for now because their very special napping arrangements will remain our little secret: no one need ever know ...

OLLIE and NINA

and... *Man's best friend*

HEY, OLLIE, THEY SAY THAT A DOG IS **MAN'S BEST FRIEND** ...

... OR **WOMAN'S** BEST FRIEND NINA – DEPENDS ON WHO HAS **DA CHEESE!**

BENTLEY

"**N**ina's got a boyfriend! Nina's got a boyfriend!"

This is how we like to tease Nina when her boyfriend comes a-courtin'.

He's a Working Cocker Spaniel who goes by the name of Bentley. He is the brownest dog you could ever wish to see: brown coat, brown eyes, brown nose … it's like he's made of 'Pure Brown!' He is lovely. We refer to him as 'Oh, Bentley!' coz our Nina goes weak at the knees whenever he swaggers onto the scene.

Shy Nina is usually standoffish with other dogs. She's nervous and timid. Not so when it comes to 'Oh, Bentley!' however. She is all over him. We don't know why, exactly. We can't work out what 'Oh Bentley's!' mesmerizing charm is. Of course, he is handsome, funny, friendly, loving and kind, but most of all he's hungry! Like, 'Feed me now, where's all the food hidden? If I don't eat soon I'm going to pass out' kind of hungry. Maybe that's what impresses Nina so much.

The first thing 'Oh Bentley!' does when he enters our house is hunt for food. He'll empty Ollie's bowl, he'll empty Nina's bowl, and then he'll empty any bowl, dish, plate or rubbish bin he can get his very brown nose into. It has to be said that Ollie, the finicky little so-and-so, just sort of picks at his meals. So, when 'Oh Bentley!' turns up ravenous, and devours every edible or inedible morsel there is to be found like it's his last meal ever, perhaps Nina thinks, 'Oh Bentley… what a *real* dog!'

They are in love. Nina loves 'Oh Bentley!' and 'Oh Bentley!' … well, he just loves food.

OLLIE and NINA

and... Bentley!

— YOUR BEST FRIEND, **BENTLEY**, IS COMING TO STAY ...

... OH **GREAT**!

... OH **DEAR**!

QUICK! HIDE ALL THE **FOOD**!

SIGH ... BENTLEY **LOVES** HIS **GRUB** ...

CHOMP! CHOMP! CHOMP!

OLLIE

... TROUBLE IS, HE LOVES **EVERYONE ELSE'S GRUB**, TOO!

OLLIE

MUNCH! CHOMP! SLURP!

RUBBISH BIN

OH, **BENTLEY**!

OOOH ... **BENTLEY**!

15

OLLIE and NINA

and...

MOTHER'S DAY!

A SPECIAL MUM

... OK YOU LOT — I'VE MADE THIS SPECIAL **MOTHER'S DAY CARD** FOR YOU ALL TO GIVE TO YOUR **MUM!**

TO MUM

HAPPY MOTHER'S DAY, MUM!

... AWWWW ...

LOVE LOVE LOVE LOVE LOVE LOVE YOU!

... IF ONLY **YOUR DAD** WAS AS **THOUGHTFUL AND KIND** ON THESE SPECIAL OCCASIONS!

17

RAIN

Nina's the one with the brains in the outfit. She watches and learns; Ollie watches and copies.

My wife was walking Ollie and Nina in the park one day when, all of a sudden, they got caught in a nasty downpour. My wife noticed how Nina huddled up close to her so as not to get rained on. It took Ollie a while to catch on to this little trick of Nina's, and huddle up, too.

I thought: "There's a nice little cartoon in that."

Please do forgive my terrible pun. Sorry.

OLLIE and NINA

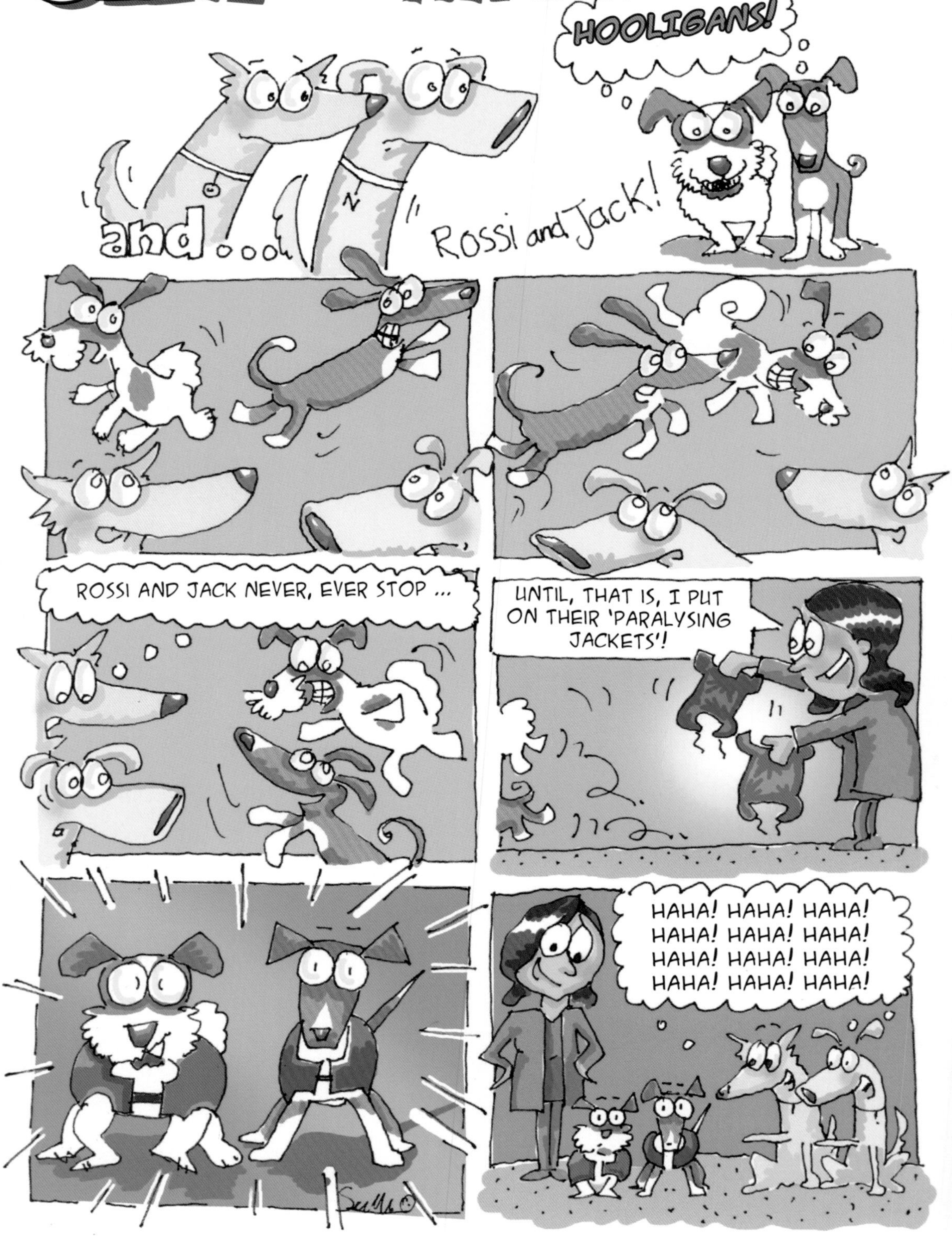

SAY 'CHEESE!'

THE VET

Oh, my goodness! The whining, the whimpering, the gnashing of teeth, the tears, chasing round the house, and coaxing from behind the sofa and under the bed: you'd think someone was going to be murdered – and that's just me I'm talking about!

I hate going to the vet, even though Ollie and Nina don't really mind at all. I think by now they trust us so implicitly, they know we will never do anything to hurt them, even if they need injections or blood samples taken. Of course, those procedures do hurt a wee bit, but they seem to know that they are necessary, and cooperate with no fuss at all.

I know that taking our beloved animals to the vet is for their good, and, of course, we will always do whatever it takes to keep them healthy and happy, no matter how much it costs. But if you think that getting me to the vet is a drama, you wouldn't want to see me coming out.

Ollie and Nina may leave the vet's healthy doggies, but I'm a broken man.

THE PONG

Because we moved from the centre of London to the middle of nowhere in a far-flung corner of Northumberland, we decided we'd get a dog, so we got ourselves an 'Ollie' (we'd get ourselves a 'Nina' a few years later).

The middle of nowhere in a far-flung corner of Northumberland was a wonderful place to be, as it turned out, especially if you had an 'Ollie.' Walks with him along the banks of the mighty River North Tyne were awesome. Treks through the forests of Kielder were staggeringly beautiful, and following in the footsteps of the all-conquering Roman army along Hadrian's Wall was mind-blowing.

I'm not too sure how much Ollie appreciated the magnitude of all this natural beauty, though: he was far too busy sniffing out stinky things to roll in. Sadly, in the midst of so much natural beauty there was always something naturally rotten for Ollie to wear in his hair: dead fish, rabbits, birds, sheep, and untold variations of animal droppings for Ollie to gleefully adorn his pelt with.

Thankfully, we were never too far from a lake, river or reservoir in which to clean off our smelly mutt.

Then, one day, to our delight, Ollie came back to us smelling rather nice for a change; wearing a delicious scent of freshly mown hay. Wow, we couldn't get enough of it, burying our faces in his gorgeous thick mane. Mmmmmm, freshly mown hay!

At about the same time as this happy occurrence, we began to notice otters in the river and on the riverbank. Thrilled to be honoured by the presence of otters on our river, we couldn't wait to get Googling to discover more about them, and their ways.

Turns out, as it happens, that a sure sign of there being otters in the vicinity is if your dog comes romping back to you smelling of freshly mown hay, which is what otter poo smells of …

Thanks for that, Ollie, you could have said.

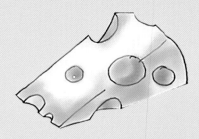

CHEESE

Picture the scene: me watching TV; Ollie watching me, and Nina watching a few slivers of leftover ham on a plate on the coffee table in our lounge.

Both dogs are obedient, and know better than to even think about stealing the leftover ham. And both dogs are clever enough to know that they don't need to steal it: the leftover ham will be theirs soon enough.

Ollie sits in front of me like a little statue. He stares hard at me, psyching me out. Okay, so now he has my attention, he begins his 'dancing eyebrows' routine. Without moving his head, his eyes dart towards the ham, and his eyebrows shoot skyward. Then his eyes flash back to me and his eyebrows fall back to earth. He might repeat this little exercise six or seven times until I get the message. "Look, Dad, there's some leftover ham over there that's in danger of being left over."

I glance over to the ham. Nina is standing rigid, simply staring at it. This is their clever, 'ham-scam.'

Of course, I give in and play their little game. "What's that you say, Ollie, some poor little slices of ham that need rescuing?"

Mission accomplished: I dangle the well-earned slices of ham into their eager, open mouths. Everyone's a winner.

They think they are so clever, our Ollie and our Nina. Don't they know that I know exactly what they're up to? As I write this, they are sitting in front of me like good little doggies, just staring long and hard at me.

Hmm … I think I fancy some cheese …

THE MUTT

There are all kinds of newfangled, fine and dandy, fancy breeds of doggie dudes out there these days: Labradoodles, Springadors, Jackawawas, Cockapoos, and who knows what else – a Staphieshep, Saushuskie, or a Dashingese, perhaps?

I suppose as Ollie is half Collie and half Saluki he could be a Colluki, and as Nina is half Saluki and half Whippet she might be a Saluppet, whatever one of those is! I never think of Ollie and Nina in those terms, though, I only ever think of them as Ollie and Nina, the daftest pair of mutts you'll ever meet. They are more like Laurel and Hardy or Morecambe and Wise, although I consider Ollie and

Nina to be even dafter than either of those comic duo geniuses.

Ollie and Nina are the perfect comedy doggie duo. Nina plays the straight guy to Ollie's clowning around. It's always him who gets up to the naughty stuff. Mind you, Nina is never far away. I wonder if Nina isn't the mastermind behind Ollie's crazy capers. He's so easily led, and up for anything at any time, anywhere.

It doesn't matter one jot to me about Ollie's and Nina's dodgy genealogy. To me they are the perfect mix of funny, happy, silly … and lovely.

36

DINING OUT

We often take our dogs out to dinner. They really love it because – even though we're not supposed to, and tell each other off for doing so – we simply can't resist slipping Ollie and Nina a tasty little morsel or two from our plates. I know, I know, we shouldn't, but we just love how much they love that we do. I've even found myself ordering a dish that I know Ollie and Nina will particularly enjoy. Now that's love!

The fun begins when I start dissecting my dinner with our dogs in mind. This bit for Ollie; that bit for Nina, and always ensuring they have equal portions. The thing is, I can see my wife doing exactly the same thing with her dinner. She pushes two little stashes of forbidden treats to one side of her plate.

"I wonder who that's for?" I say.

And so begins the illicit feeding of the doggies under the table. I didn't realize how sneaky I could be until we started this little game. While my wife is taking in her surroundings, I seize opportune moments to off-load select cuts from my plate to my hungry little pals.

Thankfully, Ollie and Nina are pretty clever when it comes to intercepting a sneaky feed. They seem to know not to make a fuss. I swear I can almost hear them stifling their giggles as they nibble on the outlawed nosh from my fingers. When I hold their treat under the table, I don't need to worry about finding a mouth to feed: it always, without fail, finds me.

My wife's method of stealth feeding is much different to mine. She tries to engage me in conversation by leaning forward, staring me directly in the eyes in an attempt to hold my gaze, while she boldly feeds our pampered pooches under the table with a portion of grub in each hand. I, of course, pretend to be oblivious to her blatant deceit.

At the end of the day, if we didn't feed Ollie and Nina under the table we'd only ask for a doggie bag and feed them when we get home. Where's the fun in that, eh?!

Of course, doing what we do is not the done thing – but still we do it.

Well, my wife does. I don't, of course – honest!

OLLIE and NINA

and ... Dining out

DON'T TELL YOUR *DAD* ...

DON'T TELL YOUR *MUM* ...

41

THE BEACH

Ollie loves the beach. When we first took him, he was totally blown away by the wide-open spaces. He'd bolt off like a loony in long, sweeping loops, pelting at full throttle with a massive grin on his face. He'd only break off from his never-ending circular gallop if he happened to see another dog anywhere else on the beach, and I mean *anywhere* else on the beach. His eagle-sighthound-eye never missed a trick. When he wanted to play, Ollie could spot any poor pooch that had the misfortune to be near (or far) from him. And when it comes to playing, Ollie can play for England.

But it wasn't every dog who had his stamina for playing. He would almost play them to death – well, into total submission, at least. The exhausted animal was only spared if Ollie spied fresh meat haplessly wandering into the OLLIE PLAY ZONE.

I'm glad to say there was never any harm done, though. But in those days, we lived on our nerves as Ollie preyed on his victims.

Ollie hasn't always loved the sea, however; it has to be said, he was very shy of the sea; very cautious – very un-Ollie was Ollie when it came to the sea. It seemed to us that Ollie thought it was a living thing. A liquid beast that was out to attack and tease him with its long, grabbing, foaming arms. He'd run at it, then away from it. He'd run alongside it barking, but he'd never run *into* it. He was far too scared of the sea, at first! But Ollie overcame his fear of the sea out of pure love, devotion – and immense bravery.

On a hot, sunny day on the beach, my wife and I decided we'd take a little dip to cool off. Ollie, being Ollie, decided that wherever Mum and Dad were going, he'd go, too. Business as usual, it seemed to Ollie … until he realised where Mum and Dad were actually heading: straight into the arms of the sea, his nemesis.

Well, that was that as far as Ollie was concerned: wild horses wouldn't drag him in there! But as we waded into the thrashing, crashing waves breaking against the shore, Ollie became a bit concerned. And as we ventured even further out, he became very concerned. By the time we were in up to our shoulders, Ollie was beside himself (he certainly wasn't beside us, that's for sure).

The poor fella was frantically running along the seashore, backwards and forwards, barking in distress. He ran from the shore's edge back to where our clothes and belongings were; then back to the shore's edge, and again back to our clothes, all the while barking and begging us to come back. It must have seemed that we were leaving him, heading off for the horizon, and never coming back.

Ollie made a decision that day which has earned him my unconditional love and devotion ever since. He decided that, no matter where Mum and Dad were going (even if it was to certain death and destruction in the dreaded sea), he was going with us. He dashed from the beach through the crashing waves, and swam the fifty or so metres out to sea to save us, or join us in whatever fate the sea had in store for us. No matter what, he had to be there with us!

As it turned out, we all had a jolly good time splashing about. Ollie quite likes the sea, now. Don't you, Ollie?

OLLIE and NINA

and... A+Z DRIVING

NEIL SUZANNE

OLLIE NINA

Sully ©

OLLIE and **NINA** and... **BLING!**

BEAMING

HEY, OLLIE, HEY, NINA, LOOK – MUMMY HAS BOUGHT YOU SOME **BLING!**

... OH, MAN, I FEEL SO **GANGSTA – BADASS** MAN!

... I FEEL PRETTY – OH SO PRETTY, SO PRETTY AND WITTY AM I ... AND ...

OLLIE, OLLIE, **OLLIE!!** GET A GRIP OF YOURSELF, MAN!

OH – ER, I MEAN – I FEEL SO ... **GANGSTER** DUDE, MAN – GRR! **BADASS!**

THE STICK

It's no good. I'm just going to have to accept it. If I throw a stick for Ollie and Nina to fetch, the only way I can expect it to ever come back is if it's a boomerang. Ollie and Nina are simply not the fetching type.

Ollie is far too harebrained to concentrate long enough to follow the trajectory of an airborne stick. Within a second of setting off after it he'd be following his nosey nose in pursuit of something rancid to roll in, or something long-dead to sneak a little nibble at.

And then, of course, there's all that 'OLLIE WOZ HERE' peeing to be getting on with. I reckon there may still be some places that Ollie hasn't 'OLLIED' yet, but not many.

So, as far as a silly old stick is concerned, unless it happens to land in something horribly smelly, or somewhere that Ollie hasn't already 'OLLIED,' it will forever be a stranger to our Ollie.

Nina, on the other hand, would need to think very carefully about chasing a stick before deciding whether or not to do so (she's a very thoughtful little dog). Nina would need to consider the pros and cons involved in retrieving a stick. I mean, what kind of stick *is* this stick? Is it a cheese stick? Is it a chewy stick? Is it a stick of great importance? If the answer to all of the above is 'NO,' then Nina's simply not interested.

However, if I just happened to be throwing 'Butchers Finest Choice' pork sausages for Ollie and Nina to fetch, I might have a bit more luck. I guarantee those flying porkers would never hit the ground, though I doubt very much if Ollie or Nina would ever bring them back to me.

Dear Reader: BE WARNED! If you ever throw a stick for Ollie and Nina, and you feel you'd definitely like back that precious stick, you'd better be prepared to fetch it yourself ...

OLLIE and NINA

and... THE BAD DOG!

BEWARE OF THE OLLIE!

GRRRRR!!!

SIGH ... WHAT ARE YOU DOING *NOW*, OLLIE?

– I'M PRACTISING BEING A *'BAD DOG,'* NINA!

NO MORE *NICE, CUTE, CUDDLY-WUDDLY* OLLIE!!

I WANNA BE A *'BEWARE OF THE DOG!'* DOG!

... WELL, NOW'S YOUR CHANCE! SOMEONE'S AT THE *DOOR* ... GO GET 'EM, OLLIE!

DING DONG!!

HELLO, HELLO! *WELCOME!* – MY NAME IS *OLLIE* AND I *LOVE YOU!* ... WE'VE NEVER MET BEFORE, AND ALREADY I *LOVE YOU* – PLEASE *DO COME IN* – I WANT TO BE YOUR *FRIEND!* HAVE YOU MET NINA? *SHE'S* MY *FRIEND TOO!* I *LOVE* YOU, I *LOVE* YOOOU!!

... PATHETIC, OLLIE, *REALLY* PATHETIC!

49

FASHION

Have you ever seen a dog do a double take? Well, that's exactly what Ollie did the day he spotted a dandy wee dog strutting his stuff in the latest doggie fashion clothes.

OLLIE: "Hey, Nina, look at that little doggie dude: reee-aal cool, eh?"

NINA: "Hmmm, not my kinda thing, I have to say, Ollie."

That's the conversation I imagine occurred between Ollie and Nina in the park that day. Ollie seemed intrigued by this new concept of dogs wearing clothes, a little too intrigued for my liking. Was he going to come out of the closet, I mean, literally come out of the closet one day wearing my clothes, or, worse still, my wife's clothes? I wouldn't put anything past our Ollie – he's a funny little dog.

Nina, on the other hand, could only tut-tut at the smug little fashionista as he went trotting by. Playing dressing up is not Nina's thing, it seems; dogs wearing anything but their birthday suits just doesn't 'do it' for our Nina.

Since that day in the park, though, both Ollie and Nina have had the odd occasion when there's been good reason to slip into something 'more comfortable.'

In Ollie's case it was just after a minor operation to remove a small cyst from his back between his shoulder blades. A patch of his coat had to be shaved so the wound could be neatly stitched, and, in order to keep the dressing clean, our vet suggested we put Ollie in a T-shirt for a few weeks. Okay, needs must, I supposed.

"Well, well, well, what do you think of that, Ollie?" my wife asked as we stood back to admire him in his new red-and-white-stripe rugby top. Ollie's face was a picture. I swear he was blushing with embarrassment and delight. It was obvious from his big, stupid grin that he loved his new clothes. He seemed energised by his new look. He couldn't wait to prance around the park showing off his cooooool hipster clobber, and we couldn't help but notice he had an added spring in his step. Was this Ollie doing his catwalk thing, we wondered?

Nina's chance came one very cold winter's day.

As usual, Ollie and Nina and I found ourselves waiting patiently outside shops on the high street while my wife did the necessary inside. I was bearing up to the cold okay; so was Ollie, but poor Nina wasn't. (She's from the sweltering climes of Malaysia, and this was her first British winter.) Consequently, the poor lamb was freezing, and shivering uncontrollably. I hugged her and rubbed her ribs vigorously to keep her warm till Mum returned. Emergency clothes shopping was obviously required.

We tried all of the jackets, in all of the colours, in all of the sizes, in all of the pet shops until we found just the right one for Nina. We knew we had the right one when the same big, stupid grin appeared on Nina's face as that on Ollie's when he had on his rugby top. She was embarrassed, delighted, and warm! I have to admit, even I thought she looked pretty cool in her warm, winter jacket.

* ❄ ❄ ❄ *

OLLIE and NINA
BEACH
and... the car!
WHENEVER WE GO FOR A DRIVE, NINA, I ALWAYS LIKE TO SIT IN THE FRONT SEAT ...
... UNLESS DAD IS DRIVING!!!
mmmmMUM!!
Sully. ©

THE DAD TRAP

Square knot, slipknot, sheet knot, half hitch knot, overhand knot: there are hundreds and hundreds of different kinds of knot, and Ollie and Nina seem to know them all.

Humans need two hands to tie a good knot with a rope; it takes two good dogs to do exactly the same with their leads. Ollie and Nina have put hundreds of dog-hours (that's about 40 hours in human terms) into practicing their knots, tangling me up good and proper every chance they get.

They do their minor knotting exercises when we're out and about, in quiet places where there's no one to witness it, and, okay, this is mildly annoying. They do their most elaborate, specialty knotting in busy, built-up places where it's extremely embarrassing, however. They like to put on a little display for the passing public, entertaining them with the 'See how stupid our Dad looks trying to unpick our superbly-tied DAD TRAP KNOT.'

Lately, Ollie and Nina are becoming very creative with their knot-tying by bringing other elements into the craft.

A tree, for instance, or a lamppost or pushchair, and, best of all, other people!

Ollie usually takes a forward position, with Nina, a few steps behind. Then they target a poor innocent third party person or object to literally rope into their tangle prank. With swift sleight-of-paw movements and devious forward, back, side step, hop skip and a jump, there we are, trussed up like a kipper. It's not a nice way to meet a stranger.

I'll spare you the details of the time they performed a particularly cruel display of DAD-TRAPPING while I was engaged in a little 'black bag duty,' if you know what I mean. It was a very cruel trick to play on me, but hilarious entertainment for the rowdy crew boozing outside their local pub. They can be very sharp, those dog leads, when you've been tied up with them tighter than Houdini. They can cut through anything – especially thin, freshly-filled, black bags ...

I've since burned those clothes, and we've sworn never to speak of that incident again.

TRAVEL

Ollie and Nina are great travellers. They love being in the car, tucked up nice and safe and comfortable on the back seat, and are no bother whatsoever.

That hasn't always been the case, mind you.

When we went to pick up Ollie from his foster home in Huddersfield, we had a nice, big estate car with an open boot, that we felt would be just perfect for Ollie. Installing headrest pet mesh guard bars to separate him from the back seats, we thought: "What could be wrong with that? Start as you mean to go on."

Well, better ask Ollie about that because he was having none of it. We must have driven only a couple of miles before Ollie had forced his way through the guard bars, bending them just enough so that he could twang himself through.

So there he was on the back seat. "Oh, well," we thought, "that'll do: he's happy, and safe enough."

But, no, that wasn't good enough for our Ollie, and with one nimble leap he'd gone from the back seat to the front, to plonk himself on my wife's knee.

"Hello, my name is Ollie; you must be Suzanne and Neil. Nice to meet you; nice car!"

In contrast, Nina wasn't the best of travellers when we first took her on. Born in Kuala Lumpur, Nina had not been outside of her pound in her two years of life, so her first time in our car wasn't a nice experience for her – or us!

She was always sick, at first, though less so with experience. We were thrilled, one weekend, when we managed to drive all the way home from a visit to the beach (about a three-hour drive) and Nina wasn't sick once. Well, not until we pulled up outside of our house, at least! We thought we'd been spared, but, no: a nice pool of sticky yellow bile awaited our attention.

I'm glad to say that Nina is never sick these days. She's a proper little commuter, and goes everywhere we go in the car, and loves it. It doesn't matter to her or Ollie *where* we go … just as long as we go!

BLACK BAG

If you spell the word 'dog' backwards you get the word 'God.'

That's pretty much how it is in our house with Ollie and Nina. They are a right pair of little Doggie Demi-Gods, and my wife and I worship them both.

Maybe that's why we go to such lengths to appease our little Dog Gods.

For example, I've had some of the worst nights' sleep ever, just because 'His Ollieness' has been lying flat out sideways on our bed all night. But rather than disturb him, I've found myself performing contortionist acts around him. And on top of everything else, he always seems to manage to commandeer the whole quilt. Ollie is not a big dog, but somehow he can take up the whole bed.

When eating out, we always go somewhere that our Dog Gods are welcome. This limits our choice, of course, but never mind: it's important that they are with us on nice occasions such as eating out. We always order something we know they will approve of. Many are the times I've sacrificed my preferred dish for something I know Ollie and Nina will like. I will order my chicken with chips rather than boiled potatoes because Nina is partial to a nice chip, you see.

We even bought our house because of its perfect location for Ollie and Nina. Open fields, forests, rivers and streams are right on the doorstep for our Dog Gods to reign over. Never mind that I have an hour-and-half commute to work: it's a small sacrifice to make, I suppose, in honour of the mighty Ollie and Nina!

We walk Ollie and Nina in all weathers. We pick up their poo like it was manna from heaven. We only go on holidays to places where they are also worshipped. We wear their moulting hair on our clothes at all times as a testament to their omnipotence. We evangelise to anyone who will listen (and even those who would rather not) about the virtues of letting a Dog God into your life.

I've got the Dog God thing so bad now that I've even taken to scribing THE STORY OF OLLIE AND NINA, an illustrated bible of their lives, in an attempt to reach out and spread the good word. DOG IS LOVE. LOVE IS DOG.

Okay, it may sound like we are a bit extreme, a bit fanatical but, nah, not really. We just love having someone to love who loves us even more! They radiate their love for us. It is perfect, it is endless, it is unconditional ... and it is for this reason we worship our daft little Gods, I mean dogs. Amen.

* ❉ ❄ ❉ *

PUPPIES

I remember all too well the first time I saw *it*. *It* was in a photograph. *It* was not a puppy. Oh, no, *It* was a Dingo! Well, that's what Ollie, the Collie/Saluki cross, looked like to me, and I wasn't that impressed, I have to admit.

Ollie is a rescue dog, and for us to rescue him we had to drive 100 miles to his foster home to check him out. My wife was beside herself with excitement, and I was right there beside her ... beside myself with trepidation. What were we letting ourselves in for with this weird-looking dog? We found ourselves outside Ollie's foster home. Ding-dong! We waited for the door to open. And when it did, Oh. Dear. Me!

We were just about to introduce ourselves to Ollie's foster Mum when he came bounding out to greet us. No need for formal introductions, it seemed. He simply pounced at me, hitting me painfully in the trouser department, causing me to gasp and double up. Ollie then gave me a big, wet kiss. (By 'kiss' I mean he stuck his nose straight into my already gaping mouth.) "What the ...?" What kind of mad, bad and dangerous to know dog was this, I wondered? But, you know what? At that very moment, as our eyes met, I was smitten. I took a better look at this Ollie-character. Wow! This was no Dingo. This was truly the Adonis of all dogs; a real beauty, like Anubis in a Collie coat.

Ollie has fine, almost feminine, facial features. His beautiful, almond-shaped eyes are rimmed with dark Cleopatra-like make-up that gives the Saluki his alternative name of Egyptian Sighthound. Ollie is also half Blue Merle Collie, so has that unique splash of mottled black, blue-grey pelt across his back. This, set off against the soft, sandy Saluki colouring, and delicate fluffy flash of wispy hair about his ears, elbows and tail, make him a very striking dog indeed. They say the camera never lies. Well, that first photograph I saw of Ollie is a case of 'Liar, liar, pants on fire.'

The first time I saw Nina was also in a photograph, and how I wished the camera was lying then. She was a pitiful sight: half-starved, and backed into the furthest corner of her cage at the rescue centre. Nina was born there, and for two years she knew nothing else. Poor Nina was terrified of everything and everyone, and it showed on her face.

That's why we decided to foster her and take her home (we lived in Kuala Lumpur at that time), just for a short while, to help her get used to people. Maybe if she learned to trust people she might one day find a nice home ...

That was a great plan, as it happened, because, after months of patience, tender love and careful attention, Nina did eventually learn to trust people, but, as it turned out, the people she learnt to trust were us, and the home she found was ours. By the time Nina was totally rehabilitated, we were totally in love with her. It was a done deal: she was our dog, and we'd never part with her.

If I were to share with you a photograph of Nina now, you'd see a beautiful Saluki/Whippet cross with big, brown eyes. You'd see a lean, mean, running machine tailored in a dappled, Bambi-coloured coat, trimmed at the ears, elbows and tail with those flashes of wispy hair, just like her best friend, Ollie. You wouldn't have to look too closely to recognise a very happy and contented dog. That first photograph of Nina in her cage broke our hearts. Those months of dedicated rehabilitation melted our hearts, and now that she is a wonderful, funny little dog, she owns our hearts, 4-ever.

I would have loved to have seen Ollie and Nina as they were when they were puppies – they must have been awesomely cute. But, for me, the first time I clapped eyes on Ollie and Nina, *that* was the day they were born.

SAY 'CHEESE!'

OLLIE WOZ HERE

Dogs: they do drop you right in it sometimes, don't they? Our Ollie certainly does, anyway.

Ollie really likes to mark his territory, which all dogs do, I guess, though none more so than Ollie. Here's how he dropped me right in it on another of his toilet-based 'occasions' ...

Heading home from a long walk with the toothsome twosome, I decided it would be rather nice to take a little short cut through the grounds of our local parish church. It's beautifully set on its own grassy island, enclosed in a circle of tall trees.

I was surprised to see so many fresh flowers on the ancient graves of people long gone, though obviously recently remembered. I stuck to the neat gravel path that meandered through the churchyard, whilst Ollie and Nina went exploring among the manicured lawns and meticulously-kept flowerbeds. What a peaceful haven of tranquillity and serenity we found ourselves in. Oh, Lord, this was the place to be on a warm summer's evening such as this one.

But as it turned out, it wasn't the place to be at all ...

The head gardener of the church appeared as if out of nowhere (that's an excellent way to arrive in an ancient parish church yard), and politely drew my attention to the sign on the latch-gate at the entrance, which informed me that 'NO DOGS' were allowed on these sacred grounds. I, of course, had seen the sign, and had, of course, ignored it. I was politely requested to put leads on my dogs, and go forth and be somewhere else ... please.

I was just about to deliver a little sermon (the theme being how Jesus surely would not have excluded any of his father's creatures from the sacred grounds of any parish church, no matter how great or small they were – 'Suffer the little doggies to come unto me' or something like that) but, before I could open my mouth and spread the good word, I noticed what the head gardener was noticing: Ollie, hunched-back and shaking like a Quaker. It wasn't fresh flowers he was laying down at the foot of that grave. It was a fresh ,.. well, we all know what it was ...

During my fulsome apology and bagging of Ollie's little offering, the head gardener was kind, and didn't say a word. He didn't need to. I did as he had initially suggested, and put Ollie and Nina on their leads, Thinking to myself "Ollie woz here, but he's going now," the three of us trooped off to be somewhere else.

On leaving the church's sacred grounds, I couldn't help but notice again the sign: 'NO DOGS.'

"See that, Ollie, see that? That means you, that does."

The look on Ollie's face was all *Mea culpa.* Bless 'im.

THE QUEEN OF 'WHATEVER'

Ruby, the Old English Bulldog, is the most chilled dog I've ever met. Ollie and Nina fuss around her, but she's just like, 'Whatever.'

It's not that she's miserable, you understand, it's just that she can't be bothered.

And it seems that nothing impresses her.

I once bought her a mad, sparkling ball that lights up and flashes amazing, crazy colours. To be honest, I bought it really because I thought it was mental, and I wanted to play with it, but just to make myself feel better about doing so I tested it on Ruby.

Bouncing it off the ground, and sending it flying all over the kitchen, it radiated dazzling, flashing colours. It was a sight you'd gladly pay money to see, but Ruby could barely be bothered to lift her head in acknowledgment, soon resuming her 'Whatever' Ruby pose on her bed at the first opportunity.

To be fair, when the crazy light bomb eventually rolled across the floor and settled close by, Ruby did deign to sniff it and snort. I think that counts as a 'WOW' from Ruby.

Whatever.

* ❄ ❄ ❄ *

73

GLEN

When I was a lad, our Glen wasn't just our Glen, he was *everybody's* Glen.

He was quite famous, known to and loved by just about everyone in and around our town. Times were different for dogs back then in the late 60s and early 70s: they had more freedom. Well, Glen certainly did, that's for sure. He was rarely on a lead: we'd simply open our front door, and off he'd go on his travels. I'm glad to say he had amazing road sense, and even used zebra crossings. I guess he watched and learned that from us kids (he was a very clever dog).

Everybody knew Glen: people we didn't even know knew Glen. He'd be greeted in the street by one of his regular human pals; a total stranger to us. If Glen could speak (I'm very surprised that he couldn't), he would have said, "Ah, Neil, this is Mr Paul. He lives down Shotley Bridge way; he always has a tasty piece of chicken for me. Nice fella."

One of Glen's duties as faithful family hound was to escort us kids to school each morning, and then he'd visit our oldest brother at his place of work. It's funny how he always turned up for the 10 o'clock snack break; just in time for a little nibble from all the workers' sandwiches. It seems Glen could even tell the time.

You might think our Glen was a bit of a tramp, but you'd be wrong. You might be interested to know that he actually had quite a fine pedigree. His Kennel Club name was 'Danvas Dice,' don't you know! And his Dad was a champion show dog. So, really, Glen was meant to be a proper show dog like his Dad, although, in truth, he was a tad too big for the ideal Rough Collie breed. And he had a dodgy, sticky-up ear that no amount of chewing gum could control.

Consequently, instead of prancing round a show ring winning trophies, Glen was destined to spend his long and happy life hacking round town doing his 'Glen-thing': winning hearts.

In spite of Glen's total freedom to come and go as he pleased, he was, in fact, a very obedient dog, who could have won the 'Mutt race' at our local country show if he hadn't been so obedient. There he was, four lengths ahead of the other doggie contenders in the 'Mutt race,' when our Mum, in her great excitement, shouted from the start line, "C'mon Glen!" Of course, Glen did as he was told, and turned round to come back to Mum. That little episode just added to Glen's fame and legendary status.

Sadly, eventually, Glen grew old and inevitably became unwell. He was stricken with seizures, and would sometimes go missing for days at a time. He would eventually stagger back home like a long-lost hero, but it was painfully clear to us all that his time had come.

I remember that terrible day – Glen's last day. It was a November morning and the first frost of that year sparkled on the ground.

Now, more than 30 years later, when I see the first frost of the year I always think of our Glen: he sparkles in my memory!

Life Is Better With A Dog

THE LONG WALK

"Okay, I'm going out now. I won't be long. I've left the TV on for you and there's plenty of water. Be good, remember you're in charge, and don't answer the door if anyone comes. I'll miss ya, bye, see you soon."

Who else talks to their dogs like this? I reckon everyone does. I talk to Ollie and Nina all the time. I like to have proper grown up chats with them. Not oochy-coochy cutesy stuff. No, I'll ask Ollie if he's particularly hungry as I'm preparing his and Nina's supper, or if he fancies his usual biscuits with a little tinned tuna, perhaps? I'll suggest to Nina that perhaps she might like to try a wee bit of sliced ham on her usual two handfuls of her favourite biscuits.

Arriving home, I might grill them about what they've been up to whilst I was out. "Hey, Ollie, have you been sneaking off upstairs to lie on the beds again? Well, Nina, has he? Has he, Nina? Oh, I see – you're not going to snitch on your big bro. Okay, I get it."

They look at me like I'm nuts, but I think that's just them playing dumb. They know exactly what I'm saying.

When I'm out walking, I often get caught talking to my dogs. You know, I'll be asking Nina, "Do you think it's going to rain, Nina?" Or I'll be telling Ollie that "We won't take the low path by the river 'cos it's too muddy," and someone will appear out of nowhere, and politely pretend they haven't heard me gassing with my mutts. One time I was explaining to Ollie and Nina about how this particular football field was the one "I scored the winning goal for our school team when I was a kid," and a voice from behind me asked which school I played for. I nearly jumped out of my skin: where did *he* spring from? He must have been hiding behind the goalposts. Talk about feeling stupid.

But just imagine if our dogs could talk back. Wow! I know what Ollie and Nina would say to me.

"Shut up, Dad, you're rambling … again!"

OLLIE and NINA

and ...

The long, long walk!

AAH .. THE **GREAT OUTDOORS** – DON'T YOU JUST **LOVE IT**, EH, OLLIE? EH, NINA? YOU JUST CAN'T BEAT IT ... THE FRESH AIR, THE WIND IN YOUR HAIR, THE SOUNDS OF THE BIRDS AND SMELLING THE FLOWERS. IT'S *SO GOOD* TO BE AT ONE WITH NATURE, DON'T YOU THINK, EH, OLLIE, EH, NINA? AAAHH ... IT MAKES YOU SO **GLAD TO BE ALIVE** ... JUST **LOOK** AT THAT VIEW, OLLIE! LOOK, NINA! – WE CAN SEE FOR **MILES AND MILES** ... WE CAN SEE THE WEATHER CHANGING! – I THINK THOSE CLOUDS ARE NIMBUS CLOUDS ... OR ARE THEY CIRRUS? OR MAYBE CUMULUS ... OH, WELL, THEY ARE **GREAT**, YEAH! COME ON, OLIIE, COME ON, NINA, *KEEP UP!* ONLY ANOTHER **5 MILES** TO GO ... *HEY, I THINK I SAW AN EAGLE!!* NATURE IS *TRULY WONDERFUL*, DON'T YOU THINK, EH, OLLIE? EH, NINA? **OKAY**, LET'S PLAY 'I SPY' ... I'LL START – I SPY WITH MY LITTLE EYE, SOMETHING BEGINNING WITH ...

WHAT'S GOT INTO DAD, OLLIE? HE'S **WALKED** OUR **PAWS** OFF AND **TALKED** OUR **EARS** OFF!

OH, DON'T PAY ANY ATTENTION, NINA – DAD'S JUST **RAMBLING** ... HE HE!

Sally©

JOGGING

Our Nina sure does love to run. And it's no wonder when you consider that she spent the first two years of her poor little life without any space at all to run. Well, it's difficult to get up to full speed in a cage at the local dog pound in Kuala Lumpur. Never mind: that's all behind her now because Mum and Dad turned up one day and set her FREE!

It took our Nina quite some time to learn what FREE! is, but she did eventually get the hang of it, and now she's excellent at it. And it's a joy to see her doing her FREE! thing.

I don't know why, but, when I see Nina running flat out across the park, I can't help humming the *Black Beauty* theme tune. She's really a very funny little dog, but, boy, can she shift! Well, she is half-Saluki and half-Whippet, after all: that's like having twin engines, I guess.

I reckon our FREE! Nina could win the Grand National: doo dee, doo de doodee doo dee doo dee … Whoop Whoop!

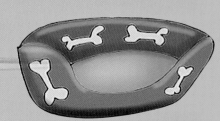

THE CAST ...

TINKA + KATJA + BAILEY + POOKEY

6'6"
6'0"
5'6"
5'0"

THE USUAL SUS-PETS ...

5'0"
4'6"
4'0"

3'6"
3'0"
2'6"
2'0"
1'6"

3'6"
3'0"
2'6"
2'0"

BRUCE + CHESTER   RUBY   GLEN   OLLIE + NINA   CHARLIE   OSCAR   BENTLEY   SAMSON + DELILAH   ROSSI + JACK

HARRY + COOPER

SEE YOU AGAIN SOON!